The Mindfulness Workbook for Athletes "The Mental Check In"

Self Reflection Workbook

The Mindfulness Workbook for Athletes "The Mental Check In"

Self Reflection Workbook

Jamel Ramsay and Dale R Horton

Title: The Mindfulness Workbook for Athletes "The Mental Check In"

Author: Jamel Ramsay & Dale R Horton

Publisher: Valiant World Media Group

Contents

Introduction

In sports, mindfulness can help you stay focused, reduce stress and anxiety, and improve your performance. It can also help you recover from injuries more quickly and prevent future injuries by keeping you aware of your body's limitations and signals.

Mindfulness is not just for meditation or yoga enthusiast. It is a practical tool that can be used by anyone, including athletes, to improve their overall well-being and performance. This workbook will guide you through the steps of practicing mindfulness in sports and help you incorporate it into your training routine.

Through the exercises and activities in this workbook, you will learn how to cultivate a mindful approach to sports, reduce distractions, and increase your mental toughness. You will also learn how to use mindfulness techniques to stay focused, regulate your emotions, and manage stress during competition.

So, let's get started on this journey toward a more

mindful and successful sports performance!

How to use this workbook

Step 1: Set aside time for daily practice.

To fully benefit from the mindfulness workbook, set aside time each day to complete the daily exercises. Choose a time that works best for you, whether it's in the morning before your day begins, during a break, or in the evening before bed.

Step 2: Start with intention.

Before you begin each day's exercise, take a moment to set an intention. This can be as simple as wanting to be more present in your training or game, or it can be more specific, such as wanting to improve your focus or manage stress.

Step 3: Complete the daily exercise.

Each day's exercise will be focused on a specific mindfulness practice, such as deep breathing, body scanning, or visualization. Follow the instructions for each exercise and take your time to fully immerse yourself in the practice.

Step 4: Reflect on your experience.

After completing each day's exercise, take a moment to reflect on your experience. Consider what you noticed during the practice and how it made you feel. Use this time to connect with your thoughts and emotions and gain insights into how mindfulness can help you as an athlete.

Step 5: Track your progress.

As you move through the workbook, take note of any changes you notice in your mental state, focus, or performance. Use the provided space to record your progress and celebrate your successes.

Step 6: Stay committed.

Mindfulness is a practice that takes time and commitment to cultivate. Stay committed to completing the workbook and integrating mindfulness into your daily routine. As you continue to practice, you'll likely see improvements in your athletic performance and overall well-being.

By following these steps and using the 26-day work-book for mindfulness for athletes, you can develop a deeper understanding of mindfulness and how it can benefit you both on and off the field.

Breathing Exercise

One of the most powerful tools in mindfulness-based sports psychology is focused breathing exercises. By bringing attention to the breath, athletes can learn to regulate their nervous system, control their thoughts, and increase their focus and resilience.

- Relaxing your body is very important when it comes to pre-performance. Let's think about what part of your body carries the tension.

- Once you Identify the area, let's start with our breathing. We will do a 6-second count deep breath. Hold your breath for 6 seconds and exhale for 6 seconds.

- Keep working on your breathing until you feel that part of your body fully relax. Please write down how you felt before your exercise:

Please   write   down   how   you   felt   after

Notes

'A Tense wire can easily break when hit with force, a relaxed one will bend and adapt."

Relaxation

Relaxation is an essential component of optimal performance for athletes. When the body is tense, athletes can experience a variety of negative effects, including decreased range of motion, impaired co-ordination, and reduced power and speed. Mindful ness-based relaxation techniques can be particularly helpful for athletes looking to calm their minds and body. One effective technique is progressive muscle relaxation, in which athletes systematically tense and release each muscle group in their body, starting from the feet and working up to the head. As athletes re-lease tension in their muscles, they can experience a greater sense of relaxation and a deeper connection to their bodies. Additionally, by pairing progressive muscle relaxation with focused breathing, athletes can enhance their ability to enter a state of relaxation and return to a state of heightened alertness when it's time to perform. Through regular practice of relaxation techniques, athletes can develop greater resilience to stress and so improve their overall performance.

Relaxing is also important when you are competing.
List 4 things that make you relax and find happiness.

1   3

2   4

Notes

"Happiness isn't a general feeling, it is as unique to a person as fingerprints."

Self-Reflection

Self-reflection is a powerful tool for athletes looking to improve their performance. By taking time to reflect on their thoughts, emotions, and behaviors, athletes can gain greater insight into their strengths and weaknesses, identify areas for growth, and develop more effective strategies for achieving their goals. Mindfulness-base self-reflection techniques can be particularly useful, as they help athletes cultivate a non-judgmental awareness of their inner experience. One such technique is the body scan, in which athletes focus their attention on different parts of their body, noticing any sensations, thoughts, or emotions that arise. Through regular practice of the body scan and other self-reflection exercises, athletes can develop greater self-awareness and a more nuanced understanding of their mental and physical states. This, in turn, can help them perform at their best by enabling them to make more deliberate and effective decisions on and off the field.

We can be very critical of ourselves as athletes; we also have coaches and parents that will try to push us to be better. List 4 things that you believe are tough or overly-critical evaluations.

List 2 things you can do to get more support with these tough or overly-critical evaluations.

Notes

"Achievable goals, when reached, will satisfy more than impossible dreams when not achieved."

Anxiety

Anxiety is a common experience for many athletes, and it can interfere with their ability to perform at their best. Mindfulness-based interventions can help manage anxiety and promote a greater sense of calm and focus. One effective technique for managing anxiety is the "three-breath hug," in which athletes imagine hugging themselves tightly while taking three slow, deep breaths. This simple technique can activate the parasympathetic nervous system, helping to reduce feelings of anxiety and promote a greater sense of relaxation. Additionally mindfulness-based cognitive techniques can help athletes identify and reframe negative thought patterns that contribute to anxiety. By cultivating a more positive and balanced mindset, athletes can reduce their anxiety and develop greater mental resilience. Athletes can develop a greater sense of calm and confidence, allowing them to perform at their best even in high pressure situations.

Anxiety oftentimes leads to negative thoughts. Positive self-talk can be very useful in keeping you in a great mindset when you are playing. Write down 4 negative thoughts that you might have when playing and for each thought, let's have one positive thing to say for that moment.

1a. Negative Thought

1b. Positive Thought

2a. Negative Thought

2b. Positive Thought

3a. Negative Thought

3b. Positive Thought

4a. Negative Thought

4b. Positive Thought

Notes

"When your greatest supporter is yourself, you are never left without positive encouragement."

Mind-fullness

Athletes may experience a variety of challenges that can impact their mental health and performance. Mindfulness-based interventions can be helpful for athletes struggling with issues such as stress, burnout, and self-doubt. One effective technique is the "RAIN" method, which involves recognizing, accepting, investigating, and nurturing difficult emotions. By bringing awareness to their emotions and accepting without judgment, athletes can begin to investigate the underlying causes and develop more effective strategies for managing them. Additionally, mindfulness-based practices, such as self-compassion, can help athletes cultivate a more positive and supportive inner dialogue, reducing feelings of self-doubt and promoting a greater sense of resilience. Athletes can develop greater emotional regulation and mental flexibility, allowing them to perform at their best even in the face of adversity.

A. Identify one thing you are struggling with in your sport.

B. What can you do to help with this struggle?

When players fall into a slump, it's best to think back to their past success; if you have trophies, medals, or ribbons place these things where you can see them every day. Remember your past success will give you the energy to push to the next success.

Notes

"Struggle is not a sign of inadequacy. It is the next step at reaching one's full potential."

Negative Thoughts

Negative thoughts are a common challenge for athletes, and they can have a significant impact on their mental health and performance. Mindfulness-based interventions can be helpful for athletes struggling with negative thoughts by helping them develop greater awareness and control over their thinking patterns. One effective technique is cognitive diffusion, in which athletes learn to observe their thoughts without judgment and recognize that they are not necessarily true or accurate reflections of reality. By creating distance from their negative thoughts, athletes can reduce their power and impact on their emotions and behavior. Additionally, mindfulness-based practices, such as gratitude and positive self-talk, can help athletes nurture a more positive mindset and reduce the frequency and intensity of negative thoughts. Athletes can develop greater mental resilience and flexibility, allowing them to overcome negative thoughts and perform at their best.

90% of the bad thoughts we have in sports never happen, however many times we spend a lot of time with negative thoughts. What negative thoughts are you having about your sport right now?

What is the percentage of these bad thoughts happening?

If the negative thought does happen when playing your sport, how will it affect your game? Will you be able to bounce back?

Notes

"Don't let the fear of what is possible, demoralize you from what can be."

Emotions

Emotions play a crucial role in an athlete's performance, and mindfulness-based interventions can be helpful for athletes looking to cultivate greater emotional regulation and resilience. One effective technique is the "S.T.O.P." method, which involves pausing, taking a few deep breaths, observing one's thoughts and emotions, and then proceeding with intention and awareness. By taking a moment to pause and observe their emotions without judgment, athletes can develop greater awareness of their inner experience and avoid reacting impulsively. Additionally, mindfulness-based practices, such as loving-kindness meditation, can help athletes foster a greater sense of empathy and compassion towards themselves and others, reducing feelings of stress and anxiety. Athletes can develop greater emotional regulation and flexibility, allowing them to perform at their best even in high-pressure situations.

Bad things are bound to happen in sports; when the bad things occur, how does it make you feel? List one emotion you have when you have a bad situation taking place.

Good things also are bound to happen in sports; when good things occur, how does it make you feel? List one emotion you have when you have a good situation taking place.

Notes

"Being able to learn from your wins and your losses creates a continuous path to success."

Confidence

Confidence is a key factor in an athlete's performance, and mindfulness-based interventions can be helpful for athletes looking to cultivate greater self-confidence. One effective technique is visualization, in which athletes visualize themselves performing at their best and achieving their goals. By creating a vivid mental image of success, athletes can enhance their confidence and motivation, and reduce feelings of doubt and anxiety. Additionally, mindfulness-based practices, such as self-compassion, can help athletes develop a more positive and supportive inner dialogue, reducing self- criticism and promoting a greater sense of self-worth. Athletes can attain greater self-confidence and self-efficacy, allowing them to perform at their best and achieve their goals.

Being confident is key to having success in your sport. Identify what confidence means to you.

A) In your own words write down what confidence means to you.
B) What part of your game do you feel most confident in?
C) In what part of your game do you feel you need more confidence?
D) What is something you think you can do to help build your confidence?
E) What support would you like from others?

Notes

"Negative thoughts thrive in uncertainty; be confident in your abilities."

Reflection

Reflection is an important part of an athlete's personal growth and development, and mindfulness-based it can be helpful for athletes looking to cultivate greater self-awareness and insight. One effective technique is journaling, in which athletes write down their thoughts and feelings about their experiences and performance. By reflecting on their thoughts and emotions, athletes can gain a deeper understanding of themselves and their motivations and identify areas for growth and improvement. Additionally, mindfulness-based practices, such as body scanning, can help athletes become more attuned to their physical sensations and develop greater awareness of their body and its needs. Athletes can reach greater self-reflection and self-awareness, allowing them to grow and develop both as athletes and as individuals.

Reflection: List 5 things you think you can improve on in your sport; also list 5 things you are happy about in your sport.

1.   1.

2.   2.

3.   3.

4.   4.

5.   5.

Notes

"Proper reflection is key as mirrors are the most unbiased judges."

Emotional Intelligence

Athletes who are in touch with their emotions and feelings can experience a variety of benefits, including greater self-awareness, emotional regulation, and mental resilience. Mindfulness-based interventions can be helpful for athletes looking to cultivate greater emotional awareness and attunement. One effective technique is mindful breathing, in which athletes focus their attention on their breath and observe their thoughts and emotions without judgment. By bringing awareness to their inner experience, athletes can develop greater emotional regulation and resilience, allowing them to perform at their best even in high-pressure situations. Additionally, mindfulness-based practices, such as body awareness, can help athletes become more attuned to their physical sensations and develop greater awareness of their body and its needs. Athletes can achieve a deeper understanding and acceptance of their emotions and feelings, allowing them to develop a greater sense of inner balance and well-being.

Being in touch with your emotions and feelings is important; circle which emotion best describes you.

Grateful	Positive	Depressed
Excited	Negative	Tired
Sad	Grit	Stressed
Mad	Joyful	Well Rested
Angry	Energetic	
Pumped	Anxious	

This week play with the positive circled emotions.

Notes

"Emotions have the power to cripple us as much as they can drive us."

Imagery

Imagery is a powerful mental technique used by many athletes to enhance their performance. Mindfulness-based interventions can be helpful for athletes looking to cultivate greater imagery skills and visualization abilities. One effective technique is guided imagery, in which athletes are led through a mental simulation of a successful performance or achievement of a goal. By creating a vivid mental image of success, athletes can enhance their confidence and motivation, and reduce feelings of doubt and anxiety. Additionally, mindfulness-based practices, such as body scanning, can help athletes become more attuned to their physical sensations and develop greater awareness of their body and its movements. Athletes can develop greater mental imagery skills and visualization abilities, allowing them to enhance their performance and achieve their goals.

Imagery in sports is like being able to see what you are going to do before you go out and compete. Have you practiced imagery? Take 15 min in a quiet place and think about the sporting event you have coming up soon.

How does this event make you feel?

How does it look?

What are some things you see happening?

Can you see great things happening?

Write down some positive things you remember from your imagery.

Notes

"Visualization is an essential step to the realization of an achievement."

Pre-Performance

Anxiety can take over your thoughts when competing; breathing is a great way to calm your mind and relax your body. Think of pre-performance, during competition, and post-game anxiety. Visualize each moment and identify where your anxiety is coming from. Once you have an idea of what might be the cause of this feeling, then start with your breathing.

Go to a safe space for you to have free thoughts and feelings.

Think of your feelings and thoughts for each section of your sport. Practice these breathing exercises:

Pre-performance- 6 seconds inhale, 6 seconds exhale for 2 min.

During competition- 6 seconds inhale, 6 seconds exhale for 2min.

Post competition- 6 seconds inhale, 6 seconds exhale for 2 min.

Notes

"When you concentrate on involuntary actions, you clear your mind of unnecessary noise."

Disconnect

Disconnecting from external distractions and focusing on the present moment is an important skill for athletes looking to enhance their performance. Mindfulness-based interventions can be helpful for athletes looking to cultivate greater present moment awareness and reduce distractions. One effective technique is mindfulness of breath, in which athletes focus their attention on their breath and observe their thoughts and sensations without judgment. By bringing their attention to the present moment, athletes can develop greater mental clarity and focus, reducing feelings of stress and anxiety. Additionally, mindfulness-based practices, such as mindful walking or body scans, can help athletes become more attuned to their physical sensations and develop greater awareness of their surroundings. Athletes can reach greater present moment awareness and enhance their ability to disconnect from external distractions, allowing them to perform at their best even in challenging situations.

The Day for Disconnection
Take a day to step away from your sport.

How does this event make feel?

How does it look?

What are some things you see happening?

Can you see great things happening?

Write down some positive things you remember from your imagery.

Notes

"Solitary reflection is the purest form of growth."

Goals

Setting and achieving goals is a crucial part of an athlete's development and success. Mindfulness-based interventions can be helpful for athletes looking to cultivate greater goal-setting abilities and focus. One effective technique is mindfulness-based goal setting, in which athletes set specific, measurable, achievable, relevant, and time-bound (SMART) goals and use mindfulness-based practices, such as visualization and positive self-talk to enhance their motivation and focus. By bringing their attention to the present moment and cultivating a positive mindset, athletes can develop greater mental resilience and persistence, helping them to overcome obstacles and achieve their goals. Additionally, mindfulness-based practices, such as body awareness and breathing techniques, can help athletes manage stress and anxiety, allowing them to perform at their best under pressure. Athletes can develop greater goal-setting abilities and focus, allowing them to achieve their full potential both on and off the field.

Goals: It's important to have a plan, so let's plan out the week and month.

What's the goal that you would like to achieve in your sport this week?

What can you do to help you reach this goal this week?

Take a minute to think about your long-term goal:

What would you like to accomplish in your sport this month?

How can you use your short-term goal to help reach your long-term goal?

Notes

"Planning is the cure for uncertainty, doubt, and fear."

Body Scan Meditation

Body Scan Meditation is a mindfulness exercise that can help you tune into your body and release any tension or stress. By scanning your body from your toes up to the top of your head, you'll learn to be more aware of the physical sensations in your body and how they relate to your mental state. This exercise can help you feel more relaxed, grounded, and present in the moment.

Lie down in a comfortable position with your eyes closed. Take a few deep breaths, and then start scanning your body from your toes up to the top of your head. Focus on each part of your body and consciously release any tension you feel. Spend more time on areas where you feel tension and repeat the process until you feel relaxed.

Notes

"Just like our minds, our bodies retain information, take inventory, and access often."

Breath Awareness

Breath awareness is a simple mind- fulness exercise that can help you calm your mind and reduce stress. By focusing on your breath and observing the sensation of the air moving in and out of your body, you'll learn to be more present in the moment and less distracted by your thoughts. This exercise can help you improve your concentration, focus, and overall well-being.

Sit or lie down in a comfortable position and close your eyes. Take a few deep breaths, and then focus on your breathing. Observe the sensation of the air moving in and out of your body, and the rise and fall of your chest or belly. If your mind starts to wander, gently bring your attention back to your breath.

Notes

"Not many things in life can be both necessary and involuntary; breathing is one such task."

Visualization

Visualization is a powerful tool that athletes can use to enhance their performance. By visualizing yourself succeeding and achieving your goals, you'll create a mental image of what success looks and feels like. This exercise can help you build confidence, reduce anxiety, and prepare for competitions or challenges.

Sit or lie down in a comfortable position and close your eyes. Visualize yourself performing at your best. See yourself succeeding, achieving your goals, and feeling confident. Visualize in detail, using all your senses. Imagine the sounds, smells, and physical sensations associated with your success.

Notes

"Winning starts in the mind; without the mindset of a winner, the difficulty is multiplied."

Gratitude Practice

Gratitude is an important aspect of mindfulness that can help you appreciate the positive things in your life. By taking a few minutes each day to reflect on things you're grateful for, you'll cultivate a more positive attitude and mindset. This exercise can help you stay motivated, resilient, and content.

Take a few minutes each day to reflect on things you're grateful for. Write them down in a journal or say them out loud. Focus on the positive things in your life, even if they seem small. This practice can boost your positivity and help you feel more content.

Notes

"Appreciate what you have in order to have what it is you appreciate."

Sensory Awareness

Sensory awareness is a mindfulness exercise that can help you stay present and mindful throughout the day. By focusing on the sensations associated with a task, like washing your hands, you'll learn to be more aware of your surroundings and less distracted by your thoughts. This exercise can help you improve your focus, attention, and overall well-being.

Pick a task you do every day, like washing your hands, and use it as an opportunity to practice sensory awareness. Focus on the sensations associated with the task, like the temperature of the water, the feel of the soap, and the sound of the water running. This practice can help you stay present and mindful throughout the day.

Notes

"We are the sum of our parts; every detail no matter how minuscule is what makes us who we are."

Affirmations

Affirmations are positive statements that can help you build a more positive self-image. By choosing an affirmation that resonates with you and repeating it to yourself several times a day, you'll start to believe in your own abilities and strengths. This exercise can help you build confidence, self-esteem, and resilience.

Choose a positive affirmation that resonates with you, such as "I am strong and capable." Repeat it to yourself several times a day, especially when you need a confidence boost. This practice can help you cultivate a more positive self-image.

Notes

"Where positivity flows, negativity can't hold."

Positive Self-Talk

Positive self-talk is a mindfulness exercise that can help you replace negative thoughts with positive ones. By paying attention to your self-talk and replacing negative thoughts with positive ones, you'll create a more positive internal dialogue. This exercise can help you stay motivated, focused, and confident.

Pay attention to your self-talk and replace negative thoughts with positive ones. For example, instead of thinking "I can't do this," think "I can do this; I am capable." This practice can help you stay motivated and focused.

Notes

"Outer peace comes from inner tranquility."

Progressive Muscle Relaxation

Progressive muscle relaxation is a mindfulness exercise that can help you release tension and stress from your body. By tensing and releasing each muscle group, you'll learn to be more aware of the physical sensations in your body and how they relate to your mental state. This exercise can help you feel more relaxed, grounded, and present in the moment.

Sit or lie down in a comfortable position and close your eyes. Tense your muscles, starting with your feet, and hold the tension for a few seconds. Then, release the tension and feel the relaxation in your muscles. Move up your body, tensing and releasing each muscle group.

Notes

"Longevity and efficiency are built off. routine maintenance."

Mantra Meditation

Mantra meditation is a mindfulness exercise that involves repeating a word or phrase to yourself. By focusing on the sound and feeling of the mantra, you'll create a sense of calm and stillness in your mind. This exercise can help you improve your concentration, focus, and overall well-being.

Choose a word or phrase that resonates with you, such as "peace" or "calm." Sit or lie down in a comfortable position and close your eyes. Repeat the word or phrase to yourself, focusing on the sound and the feeling it creates in your body. If your mind starts to wander, gently bring your attention back to the mantra.

Notes

"The power of words stretches far beyond conversation."

Mindful Breathing

Mindful breathing is a simple mindfulness exercise that can help you calm your mind and reduce stress. By focusing on your breath and observing the sensation of the air moving in and out of your body, you'll learn to be more present in the moment and less distracted by your thoughts. This exercise can help you improve your concentration, focus, and overall well-being.

Sit or lie down in a comfortable position and close your eyes. Focus on your breathing. Observe the sensation of the air moving in and out of your body, and the rise and fall of your chest or belly. If your mind starts to wander, gently bring your attention back to your breath.

Notes

"Every life begins with a fresh breath; every breath after is a fresh start."

Loving-Kindness Meditation

Loving-kindness meditation is a mindfulness exercise that involves sending love and kindness to yourself and others. By focusing on a person or group of people you care about, you'll create a sense of warmth, compassion, and empathy. This exercise can help you develop positive emotions towards yourself and others, and reduce negative emotions, such as anger or resentment. The practice of loving-kindness meditation can enhance your well-being, improve your social connections, and increase your overall sense of happiness and contentment. It can also help you develop a more positive outlook on life and promote feelings of peace and inner calm.

Sit or lie down in a comfortable position and close your eyes. Focus on a person or group of people you care about. Imagine sending them love and kindness. Repeat phrases like "may you be happy," "may you be healthy," and "may you be at peace."

Notes

"It's only through giving love do we truly understand how to receive it."

Mindful Eating

Mindful eating is a mindfulness exercise that can help you cultivate a healthier relationship with food. By paying attention to the taste, texture, and sensation of each bite of food, you'll learn to be more present in the moment and less distracted by external factors. This exercise can help you make healthier food choices, appreciate the nourishment that food provides, and prevent overeating.

Mindful eating can also help you develop a greater sense of self-awareness and mindfulness around your eating habits. By noticing the emotions, thoughts, and physical sensations that arise before, during, and after meals, you can become more attuned to your body's needs and preferences. This exercise can also help you identify triggers for unhealthy eating behaviors and develop strategies for making more conscious and intentional choices around food. By practicing mindful eating regularly, you can create a healthier and more enjoyable relationship with food and improve your overall physical and mental well-being.

Notes

"Bad habits we are groomed into, can be conquered by good routines we adopt."

Notes

Notes

Notes

About the Authors

Jamel Ramsay is an accomplished college football coach with over a decade of experience. He currently serves as the head football coach at Nassau Community College, where he has been for the past six years. During his tenure, he led the team to win one bowl game, participated in another, and was the runner-up for the D3 National Football Conference for junior college football.

In addition to coaching, Jamel is a co-owner of Port Fitness Studio, located in Port Washington, New York, where he has been providing health and fitness services to parents and athletes for over a decade. Jamel is also a leading expert in Applied Sports Psychology Consulting and is the director of Cerebral Sports. With a dual master's degree in sports psychology and sports administration from Lock Haven University, Jamel possesses a deep understanding of the psychological and administrative aspects of sports. He also brings a wealth of experience as a former Division-Two college football player and professional Arena Football League player.

Jamel has written a sports psychology workbook that emphasizes athlete mindfulness. His goal is to help athletes worldwide by providing them with practical strategies for developing mental toughness and resilience on the field, as well as connecting their minds and bodies to the game.

Currently residing in Huntington, New York, with his wife, Jessica, and his son, James, Jamel is committed to making a difference in the world of sports. For more information about Jamel and his work with Cerebral Sports, visit his website at CerebralSports.org

Dale R. Horton is an accomplished poetry and positive spoken word writer from Queens, New York. As the author of the best-selling book, "109 Positive Poems" and "Quotes to Get You Through the Day," he has received many accolades and 5-star reviews for his writing and real-world reliability.

www.ingramcontent.com/pod-product-compliance
Lightning Source LLC
Chambersburg PA
CBHW020325130626
46549CB00003B/1027